W9-AWG-439

CHECKERBOARD BIOGRAPHY LIBRARY

U.S. PRESIDENTS

The United States Presidents

FRANKLIN PIERCE

ABDO Publishing Company

BreAnn Rumsch

visit us at
www.abdopublishing.com

Published by ABDO Publishing Company, 8000 West 78th Street, Edina, Minnesota 55439.
Copyright © 2009 by Abdo Consulting Group, Inc. International copyrights reserved in all
countries. No part of this book may be reproduced in any form without written permission from the
publisher. The Checkerboard Library™ is a trademark and logo of ABDO Publishing Company.

Printed in the United States.

Cover Photo: Getty Images
Interior Photos: Alamy p. 9; AP Images p. 13; Corbis pp. 5, 14, 21, 22; Getty Images pp. 11, 25;
    iStockphoto p. 32; Library of Congress pp. 15, 16, 19, 20; National Archives p. 27;
    North Wind pp. 17, 18, 23; Public Domain p. 29

Editor: Heidi M.D. Elston
Art Direction & Cover Design: Neil Klinepier
Interior Design: Neil Klinepier

Library of Congress Cataloging-in-Publication Data

Rumsch, BreAnn, 1981-
  Franklin Pierce / BreAnn Rumsch.
      p. cm. -- (The United States presidents)
  Includes index.
  ISBN 978-1-60453-469-6
  1. Pierce, Franklin, 1804-1869--Juvenile literature. 2. Presidents--United States--Biography--
Juvenile literature. I. Title.

  E432.R86 2009
  973.6'6092--dc22
  [B]
                              2008044330

CONTENTS

FRANKLIN PIERCE

Franklin Pierce became the fourteenth U.S. president in 1853. During his term, he helped expand America. He also opened trade between the United States and Japan.

Pierce grew up in New Hampshire. He attended college in Maine. After college, Pierce returned to his home state. There, he became a successful lawyer.

In 1829, Pierce entered politics. He was first elected to the New Hampshire state legislature. Later, he served in both the U.S. House of Representatives and the U.S. Senate.

Pierce also served in the U.S. Army during the Mexican War. He rose in rank to brigadier general. After the war, Pierce became active in the **Democratic** Party. He proved himself an able leader.

While Pierce was president, slavery divided the nation. Pierce did not personally agree with slavery. However, he believed it was legal according to the U.S. **Constitution**.

President Pierce tried his best to be a strong leader. He led the nation through a difficult time in history.

TIMELINE

1804 - On November 23, Franklin Pierce was born near Hillsborough, New Hampshire.

1824 - Pierce graduated at the top of his class from Bowdoin College in Brunswick, Maine.

1829 - Pierce was elected to the New Hampshire state legislature.

1831 - Pierce became speaker of the New Hampshire state legislature's lower house.

1833 - Pierce was elected to the U.S. House of Representatives.

1834 - On November 19, Pierce married Jane Means Appleton.

1837 - Pierce was elected to the U.S. Senate.

1839 - Pierce became chairman of the Senate Committee on Pensions.

1846 - The Mexican War began in April; Pierce joined the U.S. Army.

1847 - Pierce sailed for Mexico in May, where he joined General Winfield Scott on the march toward Mexico City; on August 19, Pierce was injured during the Battle of Churubusco.

1848 - The Mexican War ended with the signing of the Treaty of Guadalupe Hidalgo.

1850 - Pierce served as president of the New Hampshire constitutional convention.

1853 - On March 4, Pierce was inaugurated the fourteenth U.S. president; through the Gadsden Purchase, the United States acquired land from Mexico.

1854 - The United States and Japan signed the Treaty of Kanagawa on March 31; on May 30, the Kansas-Nebraska Act became law; in October, the Ostend Manifesto was written.

1863 - On December 2, Jane Pierce died.

1869 - Franklin Pierce died on October 8.

DID YOU KNOW?

During his 1853 inauguration, Franklin Pierce affirmed that he would uphold the U.S. Constitution. All previous presidents had sworn this oath. However, Pierce chose the word *affirm* instead of *swear* for religious reasons. He remains the only president in U.S. history to affirm the inaugural oath.

Pierce is an ancestor of Barbara Bush, the wife of former president George H.W. Bush. She was First Lady from 1989 to 1993.

Vice President William R.D. King was in Cuba when he took his oath of office. He became the only vice president in U.S. history to be sworn in on foreign soil.

NEW HAMPSHIRE BOY

Franklin Pierce was born on November 23, 1804, near Hillsborough, New Hampshire. His parents were Benjamin and Anna Pierce. Franklin was their sixth child. He had four brothers and three sisters.

Franklin looked up to his father. Benjamin had fought in the **American Revolution**. After the war, he farmed and ran a successful tavern.

Benjamin later became involved in local politics. He served as county sheriff and a state legislator. In 1827, he became governor of New Hampshire. Benjamin taught Franklin to respect his country, his countrymen, and the U.S. **Constitution**.

The Pierces wanted their children to be well educated. Franklin first attended the local school called Hillsborough Center. When he was 11, he attended the academy in nearby Hancock, New

FAST FACTS

BORN - November 23, 1804
WIFE - Jane Means Appleton
     (1806–1863)
CHILDREN - 3
POLITICAL PARTY - Democrat
AGE AT INAUGURATION - 48
YEARS SERVED - 1853–1857
VICE PRESIDENT - William R.D. King
DIED - October 8, 1869, age 64

8

Hampshire. The next year, Franklin transferred to the academy in Francestown, New Hampshire. Later, he attended Phillips Exeter Academy in Exeter, New Hampshire.

Franklin's childhood home was built by his father, Benjamin Pierce.

FUTURE LEADER

In 1820, Pierce entered Bowdoin College in Brunswick, Maine. At first, he did not make much time for studying. Instead, he became involved in many social activities. Pierce joined literary and political clubs. He was also active in **debate** groups. By the end of his second year, Pierce's grades were the second lowest in his class.

Pierce realized he needed to improve his grades. From then on, he studied for many hours each day. Pierce quickly improved. In 1824, he graduated at the top of his class.

After college, Pierce studied law for three years. He passed his examination to become a lawyer in 1827. That year, he opened his own law firm in Concord, New Hampshire. Pierce worked hard and became a successful lawyer.

Yet, Pierce admired his father's political career. He decided to enter politics himself. In 1829, Pierce was elected to the New Hampshire state legislature. He was just 24 years old. Then in 1831, he became **speaker** of the state legislature's lower house.

Pierce's outgoing personality helped him make many friends in politics.

FAMILY AND POLITICS

Pierce continued to find success in politics. In 1833, he was elected to the U.S. House of Representatives. In Congress, Pierce did not make many speeches. But, he was a hard worker.

While Pierce was serving in the House, the country was **debating** slavery. Some states wanted slavery and some did not. People who opposed slavery were called abolitionists. They urged congressmen to forbid slavery in Washington, D.C., and new U.S. territories.

Pierce believed the abolition movement threatened peace in the United States. So in Congress, he supported the gag rules. They banned any talk about slavery in Congress. This was meant to prevent antislavery bills from being introduced. The gag rules would not be overturned until 1844.

Meanwhile, Pierce had met a young woman named Jane Means Appleton. She was from New Hampshire, too. The couple married on November 19, 1834.

The Pierces soon started a family. They welcomed Franklin Jr. in 1836. Sadly, he died as an infant. Their second son, Frank Robert, was born in 1839. Benjamin followed two years later.

Mrs. Pierce and Benjamin

SENATOR PIERCE

Pierce's Concord home is called the Pierce Manse. It opened to the public in 1974.

In 1837, Pierce was elected to the U.S. Senate. At that time, he was one of the youngest members. In 1839, he became chairman of the Senate Committee on **Pensions**.

Mrs. Pierce eventually grew unhappy with life in Washington, D.C. She wanted to move back to New Hampshire. So in 1842, Pierce resigned from the Senate. He then moved his family back to Concord.

In New Hampshire, Pierce returned to practicing law. He found great success in the courtroom. Pierce was a strong speaker, and he was well prepared for arguing his cases. In time, Pierce was considered the greatest trial lawyer in New Hampshire.

James K. Polk was president from 1845 to 1849.

Sadly, tragedy soon struck the Pierce family. On November 14, 1843, Frank Robert died. He was just four years old. The Pierces were heartbroken.

The next year, Pierce helped **Democrat** James K. Polk run for president. Pierce managed the campaign in New Hampshire. Polk won the election. As president, Polk rewarded Pierce by appointing him New Hampshire's **district attorney**.

OFF TO WAR

Meanwhile, Texas had claimed independence from Mexico. In 1845, the United States **annexed** Texas and made it a state. This angered Mexico.

General Winfield Scott

In addition, Mexico and the United States disagreed on Texas's southern boundary. Mexico believed it was the Nueces River. The United States said the boundary was a different river called the Rio Grande. The two countries could not agree, so they prepared for war. In April 1846, the Mexican War began.

That same year, President Polk asked Pierce to be U.S. **attorney general**. But Pierce turned down

Pierce led his troops from Veracruz to join General Scott's forces.

the offer. Instead, he joined the U.S. Army. Pierce helped **recruit** other men to join the army, too. Soon, he was promoted to colonel and then brigadier general.

In May 1847, Pierce sailed for Veracruz, Mexico. Soon after, he joined General Winfield Scott. Together, the generals led their troops toward Mexico City.

The Mexican Cession added more than 500,000 square miles (1.3 million sq km) of land to the United States.

On August 19, Pierce participated in the Battle of Churubusco. During the fighting, Pierce was thrown from his horse. He injured his knee and could not ride for a month. Yet, he remained with his troops.

While Pierce was still recovering from his knee injury, General Scott captured Mexico City. Mexico soon surrendered. On February 2, 1848, Mexico and the United States signed the Treaty of Guadalupe Hidalgo. This officially ended the Mexican War. It also said Mexico gave up its claim to Texas.

In addition, the United States gained the Mexican Cession. Today, this land makes up California, Nevada, and Utah. It also includes parts of Arizona, New Mexico, Colorado, and Wyoming. The United States agreed to pay Mexico $15 million for all the land.

After the war, Pierce left the army

General Pierce

and went home to Concord. There, he resumed his law practice. He also became active in the **Democratic** Party. Pierce soon became a leader in the party's New Hampshire branch. He even served as president of the state's **constitutional** convention in 1850.

THE 1852 ELECTION

Vice President King died in April 1853, after just one month in office.

In June 1852, the **Democratic National Convention** was held in Baltimore, Maryland. At this time, slavery continued to be an important issue.

The **Democratic** Party was torn. Party delegates couldn't agree on a candidate. Some Democrats wanted a leader who supported slavery, while others did not.

The delegates voted many times. On the thirty-fifth **ballot**, they added Pierce as a candidate. Pierce did not personally agree with slavery. But, he felt each state should have the right to choose slavery. Many delegates believed Pierce's position would attract more voters.

After 48 **ballots**, Pierce received the nomination. Senator William R.D. King of Alabama became his **running mate**.

Pierce ran against former general and **Whig** Party candidate Winfield Scott. **Secretary of the Navy** William A. Graham was Scott's running mate. Pierce won the election! He earned 254 electoral votes to Scott's 42.

In 1852, Pierce was called a dark horse candidate because he was a surprise nominee.

PRESIDENT PIERCE

During his inaugural parade, Pierce traveled by carriage. He was later inaugurated at the U.S. Capitol.

On January 6, 1853, tragedy struck the Pierces once again. The family was in a train wreck. Pierce and his wife were not hurt. But their son Benjamin was killed in the accident.

Just two months later, Pierce was **inaugurated** on March 4. He was still mourning Benjamin's death. However, Pierce was able to deliver his inaugural address from memory.

After the accident, Mrs. Pierce had become weak and sick. She did not attend

SUPREME COURT APPOINTMENT

JOHN ARCHIBALD CAMPBELL - 1853

her husband's **inauguration**. And for the next two years, she refused to make public appearances as First Lady. So, her aunt Abigail Kent Means served as White House hostess.

Shortly after taking office, President Pierce helped expand the nation. That year, he appointed James Gadsden minister to Mexico. Pierce instructed Gadsden to buy land west of Texas from Mexico.

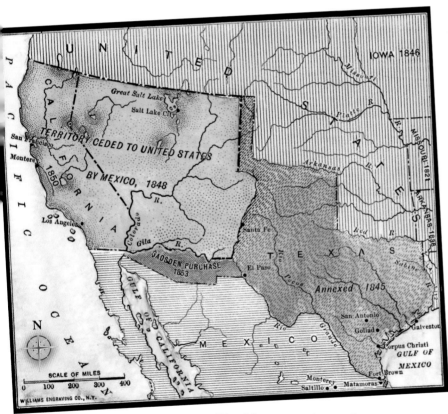

The Gadsden Purchase was a success. The United States acquired nearly 30,000 square miles (78,000 sq km) of land. Today, the purchased land makes up southern New Mexico and Arizona. In exchange, the United States paid Mexico ten million dollars.

The blue area shows the Gadsden Purchase. This land made it possible to build a railroad route across the southern United States to the Pacific Ocean.

FOREIGN AFFAIRS

Pierce continued to have success with other countries. He signed a treaty allowing the United States to fish off Canadian coasts. In exchange, Canada could trade cheaply with the United States.

Then in 1854, Commodore Matthew C. Perry voyaged to Japan. He convinced Japan to open two ports to the United States. The United States and Japan signed the Treaty of Kanagawa on March 31. It allowed the two countries to trade for the first time.

However, Pierce's luck soon changed. That same year, he hoped to acquire Cuba from Spain. In October, three diplomats wrote the Ostend Manifesto. It stated the United States might seize Cuba if Spain refused to sell.

But Americans disagreed about Cuba. Many were against acquiring it because they worried it would become a slave state. Pierce did not want to divide the nation. So in 1855, he was forced to abandon his plan.

PRESIDENT PIERCE'S CABINET

MARCH 4, 1853–
MARCH 4, 1857

- **STATE** – William Learned Marcy
- **TREASURY** – James Guthrie
- **WAR** – Jefferson Davis
- **NAVY** – James Cochran Dobbin
- **ATTORNEY GENERAL** – Caleb Cushing
- **INTERIOR** – Robert McClelland

BLEEDING KANSAS

While Pierce was president, many settlers were moving west. Under the Missouri Compromise of 1820, slavery was banned in certain parts of the country. But by the 1850s, some people wanted slavery allowed there.

In January 1854, Senator Stephen A. Douglas proposed the Kansas-Nebraska Act. It established Kansas and Nebraska as new territories in the west. It also said the territories could decide whether or not to have slavery. President Pierce supported the Kansas-Nebraska Act. So, it became law on May 30, 1854.

In Kansas, settlers quickly moved in and tried to gain control. Pro-slavery settlers set up a government in Lecompton. Meanwhile, antislavery settlers established their own government in Topeka.

Soon, people were fighting over which government was right. Violence broke out, and the fighting became bitter. This time is called Bleeding Kansas.

Congress hoped the Kansas-Nebraska Act would settle the slavery issue. Instead, it pushed the nation closer to civil war.

President Pierce recognized the pro-slavery Lecompton government as legal. So, he ordered the Topeka government to shut down. Pierce also sent troops to maintain order there.

FINAL YEARS

The fighting in Kansas slowed, but it did not stop. Many people disapproved of the situation. They no longer believed Pierce was the strong leader America needed. So, he was not renominated for president in 1856. Instead, the **Democrats** chose former congressman James Buchanan as their candidate.

In March 1857, the Pierces left Washington, D.C. Mrs. Pierce's health was still poor. So, they traveled to Europe and the West Indies. Pierce hoped the warmer weather would improve his wife's health.

In 1860, Mr. and Mrs. Pierce moved back to New Hampshire. Pierce returned to his law practice. Occasionally, he spoke in public. Pierce continued to oppose antislavery measures.

The next year, the American **Civil War** began. Pierce was saddened that the slavery issue had not been solved yet. As the war raged on, Mrs. Pierce's health continued to fail. Jane Pierce died on December 2, 1863.

Then on October 8, 1869, Franklin Pierce died. He was buried in the Old North Cemetery in Concord.

While president, Pierce showed strong leadership working with other countries. He added new land to the United States with the Gadsden Purchase. But, Pierce also faced difficult challenges at home. Many people fought over slavery, and the nation was often divided. Still, Franklin Pierce tried his best to keep the country he loved together.

Pierce's gravestone in the Old North Cemetery

OFFICE OF THE PRESIDENT

BRANCHES OF GOVERNMENT

The U.S. government is divided into three branches. They are the executive, legislative, and judicial branches. This division is called a separation of powers. Each branch has some power over the others. This is called a system of checks and balances.

EXECUTIVE BRANCH

The executive branch enforces laws. It is made up of the president, the vice president, and the president's cabinet. The president represents the United States around the world. He or she oversees relations with other countries and signs treaties. The president signs bills into law and appoints officials and federal judges. He or she also leads the military and manages government workers.

LEGISLATIVE BRANCH

The legislative branch makes laws, maintains the military, and regulates trade. It also has the power to declare war. This branch consists of the Senate and the House of Representatives. Together, these two houses make up Congress. Each state has two senators. A state's population determines the number of representatives it has.

JUDICIAL BRANCH

The judicial branch interprets laws. It consists of district courts, courts of appeals, and the Supreme Court. District courts try cases. If a person disagrees with a trial's outcome, he or she may appeal. If the courts of appeals support the ruling, a person may appeal to the Supreme Court. The Supreme Court also makes sure that laws follow the U.S. Constitution.

QUALIFICATIONS FOR OFFICE

To be president, a person must meet three requirements. A candidate must be at least 35 years old and a natural-born U.S. citizen. He or she must also have lived in the United States for at least 14 years.

ELECTORAL COLLEGE

The U.S. presidential election is an indirect election. Voters from each state choose electors to represent them in the Electoral College. The number of electors from each state is based on population. Each elector has one electoral vote. Electors are pledged to cast their vote for the candidate who receives the highest number of popular votes in their state. A candidate must receive the majority of Electoral College votes to win.

TERM OF OFFICE

Each president may be elected to two four-year terms. Sometimes, a president may only be elected once. This happens if he or she served more than two years of the previous president's term.

The presidential election is held on the Tuesday after the first Monday in November. The president is sworn in on January 20 of the following year. At that time, he or she takes the oath of office:

I do solemnly swear (or affirm) that I will faithfully execute the office of President of the United States, and will to the best of my ability, preserve, protect and defend the Constitution of the United States.

Line of Succession

The Presidential Succession Act of 1947 defines who becomes president if the president cannot serve. The vice president is first in the line of succession. Next are the Speaker of the House and the President Pro Tempore of the Senate. If none of these individuals is able to serve, the office falls to the president's cabinet members. They would take office in the order in which each department was created:

Secretary of State

Secretary of the Treasury

Secretary of Defense

Attorney General

Secretary of the Interior

Secretary of Agriculture

Secretary of Commerce

Secretary of Labor

Secretary of Health and Human Services

Secretary of Housing and Urban Development

Secretary of Transportation

Secretary of Energy

Secretary of Education

Secretary of Veterans Affairs

Secretary of Homeland Security

BENEFITS

- While in office, the president receives a salary of $400,000 each year. He or she lives in the White House and has 24-hour Secret Service protection.

- The president may travel on a Boeing 747 jet called Air Force One. The airplane can accommodate 70 passengers. It has kitchens, a dining room, sleeping areas, and a conference room. It also has fully equipped offices with the latest communications systems. Air Force One can fly halfway around the world before needing to refuel. It can even refuel in flight!

- If the president wishes to travel by car, he or she uses Cadillac One. Cadillac One is a Cadillac Deville. It has been modified with heavy armor and communications systems. The president takes Cadillac One along when visiting other countries if secure transportation will be needed.

- The president also travels on a helicopter called Marine One. Like the presidential car, Marine One accompanies the president when traveling abroad if necessary.

- Sometimes, the president needs to get away and relax with family and friends. Camp David is the official presidential retreat. It is located in the cool, wooded mountains in Maryland. The U.S. Navy maintains the retreat, and the U.S. Marine Corps keeps it secure. The camp offers swimming, tennis, golf, and hiking.

- When the president leaves office, he or she receives Secret Service protection for ten more years. He or she also receives a yearly pension of $191,300 and funding for office space, supplies, and staff.

PRESIDENTS AND THEIR TERMS

PRESIDENT	PARTY	TOOK OFFICE	LEFT OFFICE	TERMS SERVED	VICE PRESIDENT
George Washington	None	April 30, 1789	March 4, 1797	Two	John Adams
John Adams	Federalist	March 4, 1797	March 4, 1801	One	Thomas Jefferson
Thomas Jefferson	Democratic-Republican	March 4, 1801	March 4, 1809	Two	Aaron Burr, George Clinton
James Madison	Democratic-Republican	March 4, 1809	March 4, 1817	Two	George Clinton, Elbridge Gerry
James Monroe	Democratic-Republican	March 4, 1817	March 4, 1825	Two	Daniel D. Tompkins
John Quincy Adams	Democratic-Republican	March 4, 1825	March 4, 1829	One	John C. Calhoun
Andrew Jackson	Democrat	March 4, 1829	March 4, 1837	Two	John C. Calhoun, Martin Van Buren
Martin Van Buren	Democrat	March 4, 1837	March 4, 1841	One	Richard M. Johnson
William H. Harrison	Whig	March 4, 1841	April 4, 1841	Died During First Term	John Tyler
John Tyler	Whig	April 6, 1841	March 4, 1845	Completed Harrison's Term	Office Vacant
James K. Polk	Democrat	March 4, 1845	March 4, 1849	One	George M. Dallas
Zachary Taylor	Whig	March 5, 1849	July 9, 1850	Died During First Term	Millard Fillmore

PRESIDENT	PARTY	TOOK OFFICE	LEFT OFFICE	TERMS SERVED	VICE PRESIDENT
Millard Fillmore	Whig	July 10, 1850	March 4, 1853	Completed Taylor's Term	Office Vacant
Franklin Pierce	Democrat	March 4, 1853	March 4, 1857	One	William R.D. King
James Buchanan	Democrat	March 4, 1857	March 4, 1861	One	John C. Breckinridge
Abraham Lincoln	Republican	March 4, 1861	April 15, 1865	Served One Term, Died During Second Term	Hannibal Hamlin, Andrew Johnson
Andrew Johnson	Democrat	April 15, 1865	March 4, 1869	Completed Lincoln's Second Term	Office Vacant
Ulysses S. Grant	Republican	March 4, 1869	March 4, 1877	Two	Schuyler Colfax, Henry Wilson
Rutherford B. Hayes	Republican	March 3, 1877	March 4, 1881	One	William A. Wheeler
James A. Garfield	Republican	March 4, 1881	September 19, 1881	Died During First Term	Chester Arthur
Chester Arthur	Republican	September 20, 1881	March 4, 1885	Completed Garfield's Term	Office Vacant
Grover Cleveland	Democrat	March 4, 1885	March 4, 1889	One	Thomas A. Hendricks
Benjamin Harrison	Republican	March 4, 1889	March 4, 1893	One	Levi P. Morton
Grover Cleveland	Democrat	March 4, 1893	March 4, 1897	One	Adlai E. Stevenson
William McKinley	Republican	March 4, 1897	September 14, 1901	Served One Term, Died During Second Term	Garret A. Hobart, Theodore Roosevelt

PRESIDENT	PARTY	TOOK OFFICE	LEFT OFFICE	TERMS SERVED	VICE PRESIDENT
Theodore Roosevelt	Republican	September 14, 1901	March 4, 1909	Completed McKinley's Second Term, Served One Term	Office Vacant, Charles Fairbanks
William Taft	Republican	March 4, 1909	March 4, 1913	One	James S. Sherman
Woodrow Wilson	Democrat	March 4, 1913	March 4, 1921	Two	Thomas R. Marshall
Warren G. Harding	Republican	March 4, 1921	August 2, 1923	Died During First Term	Calvin Coolidge
Calvin Coolidge	Republican	August 3, 1923	March 4, 1929	Completed Harding's Term, Served One Term	Office Vacant, Charles Dawes
Herbert Hoover	Republican	March 4, 1929	March 4, 1933	One	Charles Curtis
Franklin D. Roosevelt	Democrat	March 4, 1933	April 12, 1945	Served Three Terms, Died During Fourth Term	John Nance Garner, Henry A. Wallace, Harry S. Truman
Harry S. Truman	Democrat	April 12, 1945	January 20, 1953	Completed Roosevelt's Fourth Term, Served One Term	Office Vacant, Alben Barkley
Dwight D. Eisenhower	Republican	January 20, 1953	January 20, 1961	Two	Richard Nixon
John F. Kennedy	Democrat	January 20, 1961	November 22, 1963	Died During First Term	Lyndon B. Johnson
Lyndon B. Johnson	Democrat	November 22, 1963	January 20, 1969	Completed Kennedy's Term, Served One Term	Office Vacant, Hubert H. Humphrey
Richard Nixon	Republican	January 20, 1969	August 9, 1974	Completed First Term, Resigned During Second Term	Spiro T. Agnew, Gerald Ford

PRESIDENT	PARTY	TOOK OFFICE	LEFT OFFICE	TERMS SERVED	VICE PRESIDENT
Gerald Ford	Republican	August 9, 1974	January 20, 1977	Completed Nixon's Second Term	Nelson A. Rockefeller
Jimmy Carter	Democrat	January 20, 1977	January 20, 1981	One	Walter Mondale
Ronald Reagan	Republican	January 20, 1981	January 20, 1989	Two	George H.W. Bush
George H.W. Bush	Republican	January 20, 1989	January 20, 1993	One	Dan Quayle
Bill Clinton	Democrat	January 20, 1993	January 20, 2001	Two	Al Gore
George W. Bush	Republican	January 20, 2001	January 20, 2009	Two	Dick Cheney
Barack Obama	Democrat	January 20, 2009			Joe Biden

"The great objects of our pursuit as a people are best to be attained by peace." Franklin Pierce

WRITE TO THE PRESIDENT

You may write to the president at:

The White House
1600 Pennsylvania Avenue NW
Washington, DC 20500

You may e-mail the president at:
comments@whitehouse.gov

GLOSSARY

American Revolution - from 1775 to 1783. A war for independence between Great Britain and its North American colonies. The colonists won and created the United States of America.

annex - to take land and add it to a nation.

attorney general - the chief law officer of a national or state government.

ballot - a vote. It is also a piece of paper used to cast a vote.

civil war - a war between groups in the same country. The United States of America and the Confederate States of America fought a civil war from 1861 to 1865.

constitution - the laws that govern a country or a state. The U.S. Constitution is the laws that govern the United States. Something relating to or following the laws of a constitution is constitutional.

debate - a contest in which two sides argue for or against something.

Democrat - a member of the Democratic political party. When Franklin Pierce was president, Democrats supported farmers and landowners.

Democratic National Convention - a national meeting held every four years during which the Democratic Party chooses its candidates for president and vice president.

district attorney - a lawyer for the government who works in a specific district, such as a county or a state.

inaugurate (ih-NAW-gyuh-rayt) - to swear into a political office.

pension - money for people to live on after they retire.

recruit - to get someone to join a group. A person who is recruited is also called a recruit.

running mate - a candidate running for a lower-rank position on an election ticket, especially the candidate for vice president.

secretary of the navy - a member of the president's cabinet who heads the Department of the Navy.

speaker - the head officer of a legislative assembly.

Whig - a member of a political party that was very strong in the early 1800s but ended in the 1850s. Whigs supported laws that helped business.

WEB SITES

To learn more about Franklin Pierce, visit ABDO Publishing Company on the World Wide Web at **www.abdopublishing.com**. Web sites about Franklin Pierce are featured on our Book Links page. These links are routinely monitored and updated to provide the most current information available.

INDEX